TESLA DOJO SUPERCOMPUTER
All You Need to Know About the Next Era of AI

Exploring the Technology That Could Make or Break the Future of Artificial Intelligence

Alejandro S. Diego

Table of Contents

Introduction

Artificial intelligence has long been the stuff of science fiction, a distant dream of machines that could think, learn, and adapt like humans. Yet, as we stand on the brink of a new era, AI is no longer a fantasy but a reality reshaping our world at an astonishing pace. From the way we work to how we interact with technology, AI is weaving itself into the fabric of our daily lives, creating possibilities that were once unimaginable.

In this age of rapid advancement, there is one crucial element that drives the relentless progress of AI: computing power. Traditional computers, no matter how advanced, are ill-equipped to handle the immense demands of AI. Enter the supercomputer, a technological marvel designed to process vast amounts of data at unimaginable speeds. Supercomputers have been the backbone of scientific breakthroughs for decades, from mapping the human genome to predicting complex weather patterns. But now, they have found a new calling—fueling the AI revolution.

As every tech giant races to build their own AI-driven future, the need for supercomputing power has never been greater. It is in this highly competitive and rapidly evolving landscape that Tesla has quietly been developing something extraordinary. This isn't just another supercomputer; it's a game-changing innovation poised to redefine the very concept of supercomputing as we know it. Tesla calls it Dojo, and it may very well be the most powerful weapon in the company's arsenal as it battles for supremacy in the AI wars.

Dojo isn't just a supercomputer—it's a bold leap into the future. Born from Tesla's relentless pursuit of vertical integration and first principles thinking, Dojo was crafted not just to keep up with the demands of AI, but to surpass them. This bespoke system, designed from the ground up, promises to be a digital powerhouse unlike anything we've seen before. It's more than just a tool; it's a vision of what the future of AI could be, powered by a machine that might just possess the capacity to think at the speed of light.

As you turn the pages of this book, you'll embark on a journey into the heart of this technological marvel. You'll explore the origins of Dojo, delve into the intricate details of its architecture, and discover how it could change not just Tesla, but the entire landscape of artificial intelligence. This isn't just a story about a machine—it's a story about the future, about the bold ideas and unyielding determination that could shape the next era of human achievement. Prepare to be captivated, to have your expectations shattered, and to witness the dawn of a new age in AI. This is the story of Tesla's Dojo, and it's only just beginning.

Chapter 1: The Genesis of Dojo

Tesla's commitment to artificial intelligence is not merely an aspect of its business strategy; it is the core around which the company's future revolves. From the very beginning, Tesla has positioned itself at the forefront of technological innovation, with a mission that transcends beyond creating electric vehicles. At the heart of Tesla's ambitious goals lies a deep-seated belief that AI is the key to unlocking a more efficient, safer, and smarter world.

Tesla's vision for AI is intricately tied to its goal of achieving full autonomy in its vehicles. This isn't just about self-driving cars; it's about creating a network of machines that can learn, adapt, and make decisions with a level of intelligence that mirrors human cognition. Tesla has always understood that the road to full autonomy is paved with data—vast amounts of it. The ability to process and learn from this data in real-time is what sets AI-driven vehicles apart from any other technology on the road.

This is where Dojo enters the picture. As Tesla's AI ambitions grew, so too did the need for an infrastructure that could support and accelerate the development of these complex systems. Traditional supercomputers, no matter how powerful, were not built with Tesla's unique challenges in mind. They were not optimized for the specific tasks that Tesla's AI required: processing petabytes of video data, simulating countless driving scenarios, and learning from millions of real-world miles driven by Tesla vehicles.

Dojo was conceived as the solution to these challenges—a supercomputer designed from the ground up to meet the exacting demands of AI-driven autonomy. Unlike off-the-shelf solutions, Dojo was built with a singular purpose: to be the most powerful, efficient, and scalable AI training machine in existence. Tesla's AI vision requires a machine that can not only keep up with the ever-increasing complexity of its neural networks but also push the boundaries of what those networks can achieve. Dojo, with its unparalleled processing power and custom architecture, is Tesla's answer to this need.

By creating Dojo, Tesla is not just building a tool; it's crafting the foundation upon which the future of autonomous vehicles—and perhaps AI itself—will be built. Dojo represents the culmination of Tesla's AI vision: a world where machines can learn and evolve with unprecedented speed and accuracy, ultimately leading to a future where technology works in perfect harmony with human life. As Tesla continues to innovate, Dojo will play a crucial role in driving that innovation forward, ensuring that Tesla remains at the cutting edge of AI and autonomy.

The initial idea behind Dojo was born out of necessity—a response to the immense computational demands that Tesla's AI ambitions placed on existing technology. As Tesla's vision for full autonomy began to take shape, it quickly became apparent that traditional computing infrastructure was insufficient for the task. Training the sophisticated neural networks required for autonomous driving involves processing vast amounts of data, particularly video data from the millions of miles driven by Tesla vehicles. This level of data processing and model training demands a scale and efficiency that few supercomputers could offer.

The concept of Dojo emerged from Tesla's recognition that it needed a supercomputer designed specifically for AI training, one that could handle the enormous datasets involved in real-time with unprecedented speed and efficiency. Tesla's approach to building Dojo was guided by two key principles: vertical integration and first principles thinking. Vertical integration meant that Tesla would control every aspect of Dojo's design and manufacturing, ensuring that the system was optimized specifically for Tesla's needs. First principles thinking allowed Tesla to reimagine what a supercomputer could be, unbound by the limitations of existing technologies.

The development of Dojo was a process that spanned several years, during which Tesla's AI team worked to bring the concept to reality. It began with the decision to design a custom system on a chip (SoC), which would serve as the building block for Dojo. This chip, known as the D1, was engineered to handle the parallel processing tasks required for AI training with extraordinary efficiency. Unlike conventional supercomputers that rely on large, interconnected processors, the D1 chip was designed to minimize bottlenecks by integrating all necessary components onto a single piece of silicon.

As the concept evolved, Tesla's engineers began to develop the idea of Dojo tiles—modules that combined multiple D1 chips into a single, powerful unit. These tiles could then be integrated into larger systems, scaling up to create a supercomputer capable of handling the most demanding AI workloads. The flexibility and scalability of this design were key to Dojo's development, allowing Tesla to build a system that could grow and evolve alongside its AI ambitions.

The journey from concept to reality was not without its challenges. Developing a supercomputer from scratch required Tesla to push the boundaries of what was technologically possible, often venturing into uncharted territory. But through relentless innovation and a commitment to their vision, Tesla's AI team succeeded in transforming Dojo from a bold idea into a tangible, functional system.

Today, Dojo stands as a testament to Tesla's ability to turn visionary concepts into reality. It represents not just a technological achievement, but a foundational element of Tesla's strategy to lead the world into an era where AI and autonomous systems are integral to daily life. The development of Dojo underscores Tesla's commitment to pushing the limits of innovation, creating a supercomputer that is not only a tool for today's challenges but a platform for the future.

The need for Dojo arose from Tesla's relentless pursuit of achieving true autonomy in its vehicles—a goal that required an unprecedented level of compute power. As Tesla advanced its AI models, particularly those powering its Full Self-Driving (FSD) system, it became clear that existing supercomputing solutions were not sufficient to meet the growing demands of AI training. The sheer volume of data generated by Tesla's fleet, combined with the complexity of the neural networks required to process and learn from this data, necessitated a new approach to computing.

One of the primary reasons Tesla felt compelled to create its own supercomputer was the need for a system optimized specifically for its unique requirements. Training AI models for autonomous driving is an extraordinarily complex task that involves processing petabytes of video data, running millions of simulations, and refining algorithms in real-time. This process demands a supercomputer that can not only handle massive amounts of data but do so with extreme efficiency and speed. Traditional supercomputers, while powerful, were not designed with these specific tasks in mind. They were often built for general-purpose scientific computing, not the specialized needs of AI-driven autonomy.

Another driving factor behind the creation of Dojo was Tesla's commitment to vertical integration. By developing its own supercomputer, Tesla could ensure that every aspect of the system was tailored to its specific needs, eliminating the inefficiencies and limitations that come with relying on third-party solutions. Vertical integration also allowed Tesla to control costs more effectively, reducing the financial burden of purchasing and maintaining external hardware, such as the expensive GPUs from Nvidia that Tesla had been using. Instead of being dependent on an external supplier, Tesla could create a system that was perfectly aligned with its AI goals.

The rising demand for compute power in AI training was another significant factor. As AI models become more complex, the need for more powerful and scalable computing infrastructure has grown exponentially. This demand is not limited to Tesla; it's a challenge faced by every tech company invested in AI. However, Tesla's approach to AI, particularly its focus on real-time processing of vast amounts of visual data from its vehicles, pushed the limits of what conventional supercomputers could offer. To stay ahead in the race for AI-driven autonomy, Tesla needed a solution that could scale with its ambitions—a solution that traditional supercomputers could not provide.

Dojo was conceived as Tesla's answer to these challenges. It was designed to be a supercomputer that could not only meet the current demands of AI training but also scale to accommodate future growth. With Dojo, Tesla sought to create a system that was not just powerful but also flexible and efficient, capable of evolving alongside the AI models it was designed to train. By building Dojo, Tesla ensured that it had the compute power necessary to continue pushing the boundaries of what AI could achieve, particularly in the realm of autonomous driving.

In essence, the need for Dojo was driven by Tesla's determination to maintain its leadership in AI and autonomy. The creation of this supercomputer was a strategic move to ensure that Tesla had the technological foundation necessary to support its ambitious goals. Dojo represents not just a response to the challenges of today but a proactive step toward the future, positioning Tesla at the forefront of the next era of AI development.

Chapter 2: The Evolution of Supercomputers

The history of supercomputers is a tale of relentless innovation, driven by the ever-growing need to process vast amounts of data at unprecedented speeds. The journey began in the 1960s, a time when the concept of a computer that could perform billions of calculations per second was little more than a dream. The first supercomputers were designed to tackle the most complex scientific problems of the day, from weather forecasting to nuclear simulations, tasks that required computational power far beyond the capabilities of standard computers.

One of the earliest and most iconic supercomputers was the CDC 6600, introduced in 1964 by Control Data Corporation. Often regarded as the world's first true supercomputer, the CDC 6600 was the brainchild of Seymour Cray, a visionary engineer who would later become synonymous with supercomputing. The CDC 6600 could execute three million instructions per second, a remarkable feat at the time, making it the fastest computer in the world. It was used primarily for scientific research, particularly in fields like physics and meteorology, where the ability to process large datasets and run complex simulations was essential.

The 1970s and 1980s saw the rise of even more powerful supercomputers, as demand for high-performance computing grew in tandem with advancements in technology. Seymour Cray continued to lead the charge with the development of the Cray-1 in 1976, a machine that became the gold standard in supercomputing. The Cray-1 was used by governments and research institutions around the world to perform tasks such as nuclear weapons design, fluid dynamics simulations, and other high-stakes scientific research. Its success solidified the role of supercomputers as indispensable tools for solving the most demanding computational problems.

As we moved into the 1990s and early 2000s, supercomputers continued to evolve, becoming more powerful and more widely used across various scientific disciplines. The advent of parallel processing, where multiple processors work on different parts of a problem simultaneously, was a game-changer. This technology allowed supercomputers to achieve even greater speeds and handle more complex simulations. Machines like the IBM Blue Gene and the Earth Simulator, developed in Japan, pushed the boundaries of what was possible, enabling breakthroughs in fields ranging from genomics to climate modeling.

Traditionally, supercomputers were the domain of government agencies, research laboratories, and large corporations, used for tasks that required immense computational resources. These machines played a critical role in advancing our understanding of the natural world, from predicting the weather to mapping the human genome. They were used to model everything from the behavior of subatomic particles to the effects of climate change, helping scientists make sense of complex phenomena that would be impossible to study otherwise.

However, as the 21st century progressed, the role of supercomputers began to expand beyond traditional scientific research. The rise of artificial intelligence (AI) introduced a new frontier for supercomputing, one that required processing power on a scale never before imagined. The need to train AI models, particularly those used in machine learning and deep learning, created unprecedented demand for high-performance computing resources. Supercomputers that were once used primarily for scientific simulations were now being repurposed to train neural networks, driving innovations in fields as diverse as healthcare, finance, and, of course, autonomous driving.

This shift in the role of supercomputers marks a new chapter in their history, one where the lines between scientific research and technological innovation are increasingly blurred. As we look to the future, supercomputers will continue to play a pivotal role, not just in advancing our understanding of the world, but in shaping the technologies that will define our lives in the decades to come. Tesla's Dojo is the latest evolution in this storied history, a supercomputer designed not just to keep pace with the demands of AI, but to set a new standard for what is possible in the age of intelligent machines.

The transition from niche scientific applications to mainstream AI development has marked a profound shift in the supercomputing landscape, fundamentally altering the way these powerful machines are designed, built, and utilized. For decades, supercomputers were the exclusive tools of researchers and scientists, primarily used to tackle highly specialized tasks that required extraordinary computational power. These tasks included modeling complex physical phenomena, simulating nuclear explosions, and decoding the human genome—endeavors that pushed the limits of what was technologically possible.

However, as artificial intelligence began to emerge as a transformative force in the early 21st century, the role of supercomputers started to evolve. AI, particularly in its subfields of machine learning and deep learning, presented new challenges and opportunities that traditional computing infrastructures struggled to meet. The process of training AI models, especially those used in deep learning, requires immense computational resources. These models are built by feeding large amounts of data into neural networks, which then learn to recognize patterns, make decisions, and improve over time. The more data and processing power available, the better these models can perform.

Initially, AI development was confined to research labs and academic institutions, much like the early days of supercomputing. But as AI technologies proved their potential in a wide range of applications—from image and speech recognition to natural language processing and autonomous vehicles—there was a growing demand to scale these innovations. Companies across various industries began to recognize the value of AI in solving complex problems, optimizing operations, and creating new products and services. This burgeoning interest in AI drove the need for more powerful and accessible supercomputing capabilities, beyond what traditional scientific research demanded.

The supercomputing landscape began to transform as a result. The design of supercomputers started to shift from being primarily focused on solving specific scientific problems to being optimized for the parallel processing tasks required in AI training. Graphics Processing Units (GPUs), originally developed for rendering video games, became the hardware of choice for AI workloads due to their ability to handle the kind of parallel computations necessary for training neural networks. This led to a surge in demand for GPUs, and companies like Nvidia quickly became central players in the AI revolution.

Supercomputers that were once built to model weather systems or simulate nuclear reactions were now being re-engineered to train AI models on a massive scale. The focus on AI also brought about a new emphasis on efficiency and scalability, as the sheer volume of data involved in AI training required systems that could be expanded and adapted as needed. This demand for flexibility and power pushed supercomputing technology forward, leading to innovations such as system-on-chip designs, wafer-scale integration, and the development of AI-specific supercomputers like Tesla's Dojo.

The impact of this AI-driven shift extends beyond just the technology. It has democratized access to supercomputing power, making it a vital resource not just for governments and large research institutions, but also for tech companies, startups, and even individual developers. Cloud computing platforms began offering AI training as a service, allowing more people than ever before to harness the power of supercomputing for their own AI projects. This has led to an explosion of AI applications in everything from healthcare and finance to entertainment and autonomous driving.

In this new landscape, supercomputers are no longer just tools for scientific discovery; they are engines of innovation, driving the development of technologies that are rapidly becoming part of our everyday lives. The AI shift has transformed supercomputing from a niche resource into a mainstream necessity, integral to the future of industries across the globe. As AI continues to evolve and expand, the supercomputing landscape will undoubtedly keep advancing, with machines like Tesla's Dojo at the forefront of this new era.

Parallel computing is a concept that lies at the heart of modern supercomputers, enabling them to perform at the extraordinary levels required for tasks like AI training, scientific simulations, and complex data analysis. At its core, parallel computing is about dividing a large problem into smaller, more manageable pieces, which can then be processed simultaneously by multiple computing units. This approach dramatically increases the speed and efficiency of computations, allowing supercomputers to tackle problems that would be impossible for a single processor to handle alone.

To understand how parallel computing works, imagine an F1 pit crew during a race. When a race car pulls into the pit stop, there isn't just one mechanic working on the car; instead, a team of specialists simultaneously attacks the car from different angles. One person changes the tires, another refuels the car, someone else adjusts the wing, and so on. Each crew member has a specific task, and they all work in unison to get the car back on the track as quickly as possible. The entire process is completed in a matter of seconds because the tasks are done in parallel, rather than one after the other.

In a similar way, parallel computing allows a supercomputer to break down a large computational task into smaller subtasks, which are then distributed across multiple processors. Instead of one processor attempting to solve a problem sequentially—one step at a time—many processors work on different parts of the problem at the same time. This division of labor significantly reduces the time it takes to complete the task, much like how the F1 pit crew can service a car faster by working together.

The importance of parallel computing in modern supercomputers cannot be overstated. As the complexity of tasks, particularly in AI development, has grown, so too has the need for computing power that can scale to meet these demands. Training AI models, for instance, involves processing vast amounts of data, often in the form of high-resolution images, video frames, or complex datasets. To train a neural network effectively, the data must be fed into the system, processed, and analyzed in real-time. This requires a supercomputer that can handle millions of calculations per second, something only possible through parallel computing.

Graphics Processing Units (GPUs), commonly used in parallel computing, are particularly well-suited for these tasks. Originally designed for rendering images and video in parallel, GPUs have become the workhorses of AI training because they can process multiple data streams simultaneously. This capability makes them ideal for running the numerous calculations required by neural networks, which need to process and learn from data in parallel to identify patterns and make predictions.

In modern supercomputers like Tesla's Dojo, parallel computing is taken to the next level. Dojo's architecture is specifically designed to maximize parallel processing efficiency, enabling it to train AI models faster and more effectively than traditional systems. By leveraging parallel computing, Dojo can process massive amounts of data simultaneously, reducing the time it takes to train complex AI models and allowing Tesla to accelerate the development of its autonomous driving technology.

Parallel computing is what makes supercomputers truly super. It's the secret sauce that allows these machines to perform the kinds of tasks that are reshaping our world, from advancing scientific research to powering the AI revolution. Just as the F1 pit crew relies on teamwork to get the job done quickly, parallel computing relies on multiple processors working together in harmony to achieve computational feats that would be impossible for a single processor alone.

Chapter 3: Nvidia's Dominance and Tesla's Challenge

Nvidia has established itself as the undisputed leader in GPU (Graphics Processing Unit) technology, a position that has made it a critical player in the development and advancement of artificial intelligence (AI). Originally known for its powerful graphics cards used in gaming and visual computing, Nvidia's role in the tech industry has dramatically expanded as the demand for AI capabilities has surged. Today, Nvidia's GPUs are the backbone of AI training and deployment across a wide range of industries, from autonomous vehicles to healthcare and finance.

The journey of Nvidia from a company focused on gaming to a pivotal force in AI began with its recognition of the potential of GPUs beyond just rendering graphics. Unlike traditional CPUs (Central Processing Units), which are designed to handle a wide range of general-purpose tasks, GPUs are specialized processors that excel at performing many calculations simultaneously. This parallel processing capability is what makes GPUs particularly well-suited for AI workloads, where large amounts of data need to be processed in parallel to train neural networks effectively.

As AI development gained momentum in the early 2010s, researchers and engineers quickly realized that GPUs could significantly accelerate the training of deep learning models. Nvidia, with its industry-leading GPU technology, was in the perfect position to capitalize on this growing demand. The company began to optimize its GPUs specifically for AI and machine learning tasks, leading to the creation of powerful GPUs like the Tesla K80 and the more recent A100 and H100 models. These GPUs became the industry standard for AI training, providing the necessary compute power to handle the massive datasets and complex algorithms that drive modern AI systems.

Nvidia's GPUs are designed to support the kind of parallel processing required for AI tasks, making them indispensable for training deep learning models. In AI training, vast amounts of data—such as images, text, or video—are fed into neural networks, which then learn to recognize patterns, make predictions, and improve over time. This process requires immense computational power, which Nvidia's GPUs provide by allowing multiple data streams to be processed simultaneously. As a result, AI models can be trained more quickly and with greater accuracy, enabling breakthroughs in areas such as natural language processing, computer vision, and autonomous driving.

The significance of Nvidia's role in AI development is perhaps most evident in the way it has become a cornerstone of the AI infrastructure for tech giants and startups alike. Companies like Google, Amazon, and Microsoft rely on Nvidia GPUs for their AI-powered services, while research institutions and universities use Nvidia's technology to push the boundaries of what AI can achieve. The company's GPUs have become so integral to AI that Nvidia's stock price has soared, reflecting the market's recognition of its crucial role in the future of technology.

In the context of Tesla, Nvidia's GPUs have played a vital role in the development of the company's Full Self-Driving (FSD) technology. Tesla has used thousands of Nvidia GPUs in its data centers to train its AI models, which are responsible for interpreting the vast amounts of data collected by its vehicles' sensors. These models must be trained to recognize objects, make decisions, and navigate complex environments—all tasks that require the kind of parallel processing power that Nvidia's GPUs provide. Tesla's reliance on Nvidia hardware highlights the company's critical role in the AI ecosystem, even as Tesla works to develop its own supercomputer, Dojo.

Nvidia's leadership in GPU technology has not only enabled the rapid advancement of AI but has also positioned the company at the center of the AI revolution. As AI continues to evolve and expand into new areas, Nvidia's GPUs will remain a key component of the infrastructure that powers these innovations. The company's ability to adapt its technology to meet the specific needs of AI development has cemented its status as a leader in the industry, ensuring that Nvidia will continue to play a crucial role in shaping the future of AI.

Tesla's use of Nvidia's A100 and H100 GPUs has been pivotal in the development of its AI models, particularly those powering its Full Self-Driving (FSD) system. As Tesla pushed forward in its quest to achieve full autonomy, the need for massive computational power became increasingly clear. The company required hardware capable of processing the enormous volumes of data generated by its fleet of vehicles, data that would be used to train neural networks responsible for interpreting real-world driving scenarios. Nvidia's GPUs, with their unparalleled parallel processing capabilities, were the ideal solution for this task.

The Nvidia A100, introduced in 2020, quickly became the gold standard for AI training. This GPU was designed specifically for high-performance computing and AI workloads, offering a combination of speed, efficiency, and scalability that was unmatched at the time. Tesla adopted the A100 in large numbers, deploying nearly 6,000 of these GPUs in its data centers to support the training of its AI models. The A100's ability to handle multiple data streams simultaneously made it an invaluable tool for Tesla as it refined its FSD technology, enabling the company to process vast amounts of video and sensor data in real-time.

Building on the success of the A100, Nvidia later introduced the H100, a next-generation GPU that further enhanced the capabilities of AI training systems. The H100 brought even greater performance improvements, with faster processing speeds and more efficient power usage, making it an essential component in Tesla's continued efforts to advance its autonomous driving technology. By leveraging Nvidia's GPUs, Tesla was able to accelerate the training of its AI models, reducing the time required to iterate and improve the systems that would ultimately guide its vehicles on the road.

However, despite the success of Nvidia's GPUs in supporting Tesla's AI development, the company recognized that relying solely on external hardware presented limitations. As Tesla's AI ambitions grew, so too did the need for a computing infrastructure that was not just powerful but also perfectly aligned with the specific demands of its AI workloads. This realization led Tesla to embark on the development of its own supercomputer, known as Dojo.

The motivation behind Dojo was rooted in Tesla's commitment to vertical integration and first principles thinking—two core philosophies that have guided the company's approach to innovation. Vertical integration, the practice of bringing as much of the production process as possible under one roof, has long been a cornerstone of Tesla's business strategy. By controlling the design and manufacturing of key components in-house, Tesla ensures that its products are optimized for performance, cost-efficiency, and scalability. In the case of AI training, vertical integration meant developing a supercomputer that was custom-built to meet Tesla's unique needs, rather than relying on off-the-shelf solutions from external suppliers like Nvidia.

First principles thinking, another key element of Tesla's innovation strategy, involves breaking down problems to their most fundamental truths and building solutions from the ground up. Rather than modifying existing technology to suit its needs, Tesla chose to reimagine what a supercomputer could be, designing Dojo from scratch with the specific goal of training AI models for autonomous driving. This approach allowed Tesla to create a system that was not only more efficient but also more flexible and scalable than traditional supercomputing solutions.

Dojo was conceived as a supercomputer that could handle the immense demands of AI training at a level that Nvidia's GPUs, despite their strengths, could not fully address. By developing its own hardware, Tesla gained the ability to optimize every aspect of the system, from the processing units to the data transfer mechanisms, ensuring that Dojo could operate at peak efficiency for the tasks at hand. This level of control was crucial for Tesla as it sought to push the boundaries of what AI could achieve, particularly in the context of autonomous driving.

In essence, while Nvidia's A100 and H100 GPUs played a critical role in advancing Tesla's AI models, the decision to develop Dojo was driven by Tesla's desire to take its AI capabilities to the next level. By creating a supercomputer that was purpose-built for its specific needs, Tesla aimed to achieve a level of performance and efficiency that would be difficult, if not impossible, to attain using off-the-shelf hardware. Dojo represents Tesla's vision of the future—one where AI is not just a tool, but a transformative force that requires equally transformative technology to fully realize its potential.

Chapter 4: The Architecture of Dojo

A System on a Chip (SoC) is an integrated circuit that consolidates all the essential components of a computer or electronic system onto a single chip of silicon. This compact design includes the central processing unit (CPU), memory, input/output ports, and other necessary functions, all within one unified platform. The concept of SoC represents a significant leap in computing technology, particularly in terms of efficiency and speed, as it minimizes the physical space required for complex computing tasks while optimizing the way these tasks are performed.

The primary advantage of an SoC lies in its ability to streamline the computing process. In traditional computer architectures, different components—such as the CPU, memory, and input/output interfaces—are often separate and connected by buses and wires. Each time data is transferred between these components, there is a potential slowdown due to the physical distance the signals must travel, as well as the energy lost in the process. This can create bottlenecks, limiting the overall speed and efficiency of the system.

By integrating all these components into a single chip, an SoC eliminates many of these inefficiencies. The close proximity of components within an SoC allows for faster data transfer and reduces latency, as signals no longer have to travel across different chips or through long connections. This compact integration also lowers the energy consumption of the system, as there are fewer points of resistance where energy can be lost. The result is a more efficient, faster, and more power-effective computing system.

In the context of AI and advanced computing, the benefits of an SoC are particularly valuable. AI workloads often involve processing large amounts of data in real-time, requiring both high speed and high efficiency to operate effectively. An SoC is designed to handle these tasks by enabling rapid communication between the processing unit, memory, and other components, ensuring that the system can keep up with the demands of AI training and inference.

Tesla's Dojo supercomputer, for example, utilizes SoC technology to achieve its high performance. The Dojo SoC is specifically designed to handle the parallel processing tasks required for AI workloads, integrating everything needed for computing onto a single chip. This allows Dojo to process vast amounts of data quickly and efficiently, which is critical for training the complex neural networks used in Tesla's Full Self-Driving (FSD) system.

Moreover, the SoC design in Dojo contributes to the system's scalability. Multiple SoCs can be combined into larger units, such as tiles and racks, creating a powerful supercomputing cluster without the need for complex wiring or interconnects. This modular approach not only enhances the speed and efficiency of the system but also allows Tesla to scale Dojo's capabilities as needed, supporting the ever-increasing demands of AI development.

In summary, a System on a Chip (SoC) is a revolutionary approach to computing that integrates all necessary components onto a single silicon chip, dramatically enhancing efficiency and speed. By reducing latency, minimizing energy loss, and optimizing data transfer, SoCs provide the foundation for high-performance computing systems like Tesla's Dojo, which require unparalleled processing power to meet the challenges of modern AI workloads.

Dojo's design and structure are a testament to Tesla's innovative approach to solving the challenges posed by AI training at scale. From the individual chips that serve as the building blocks of the system to the sophisticated architecture that integrates these chips into larger units, Dojo is engineered to maximize efficiency, speed, and scalability in a way that traditional supercomputers struggle to achieve.

At the heart of Dojo is the custom-designed Dojo chip, a powerful System on a Chip (SoC) specifically built to handle the parallel processing tasks required for AI workloads. Each Dojo chip is designed to perform a vast number of calculations simultaneously, making it ideally suited for the kind of data-intensive tasks involved in training neural networks. The Dojo chip integrates all necessary computing components onto a single piece of silicon, reducing latency, improving energy efficiency, and allowing for rapid data transfer between its internal elements.

But the real genius of Dojo's design lies in how these individual chips are combined to form a larger, more powerful computing system. Multiple Dojo chips are fused together to create what is known as a Dojo tile. A single Dojo tile consists of 25 interconnected Dojo chips, working in unison as a single computational unit. This integration is crucial because it allows the chips to operate in a highly parallel fashion, with each chip handling a portion of the workload while communicating seamlessly with its neighbors. The result is a dramatic increase in processing power without the bottlenecks that typically occur in more traditional architectures where separate components are connected via external buses and wiring.

The tile itself is a self-sufficient module, complete with its own power supply, cooling system, and data transfer mechanisms. This modularity is one of Dojo's key strengths, as it allows Tesla to scale the system efficiently. By combining multiple tiles, Tesla can build increasingly powerful computing units. For example, six Dojo tiles can be integrated into a single rack unit, and two racks can be combined to create a cabinet. This hierarchical structure means that Dojo's computational power can be scaled up or down depending on the specific needs of a given task, providing unparalleled flexibility in AI training.

Dojo's unique design directly supports parallel computing, which is essential for the kind of workloads Tesla's AI systems require. By arranging the Dojo chips in a grid-like pattern within each tile and then stacking these tiles into racks, Tesla ensures that data can be processed in parallel across multiple chips and tiles with minimal delay. This design allows Dojo to handle the enormous amounts of data generated by Tesla's vehicles, process it in real-time, and continuously refine the AI models that power the company's Full Self-Driving (FSD) technology.

The initial version of Dojo, often referred to as Dojo Version 1, was a groundbreaking achievement in itself. The decision to integrate 25 Dojo chips into a single tile was based on the need to create a computational unit that could deliver high performance while remaining compact and efficient. This design allowed Tesla to pack a tremendous amount of processing power into a relatively small footprint, which was crucial for the system's scalability.

One of the main benefits of the 25-chip tile design is its ability to process large datasets more quickly and efficiently than traditional supercomputers. By distributing the workload across multiple chips within the tile, Dojo Version 1 can perform the parallel computations necessary for AI training at a much faster rate. This efficiency is further enhanced by the tile's integrated cooling and power systems, which ensure that each chip operates at optimal performance without overheating or energy wastage.

Additionally, the modular nature of Dojo Version 1 meant that Tesla could deploy the system incrementally, adding more tiles and racks as needed to meet the growing demands of AI training. This flexibility was crucial as Tesla scaled up its efforts to develop autonomous driving technology, allowing the company to continuously expand Dojo's capabilities without the need for a complete system overhaul.

In summary, Dojo's unique design, from individual chips to tiles and racks, is a masterclass in parallel computing architecture. The integration of 25 Dojo chips into a single tile in Dojo Version 1 provided

Tesla with a scalable, efficient, and powerful tool to drive its AI development forward. This innovative approach not only addressed the immediate needs of Tesla's AI workloads but also laid the groundwork for future versions of Dojo, each iteration building on the strengths of its predecessor to push the boundaries of what supercomputing can achieve in the realm of artificial intelligence.

Chapter 5: The Leap to Dojo Version 2

The evolution from the D1 chip to the D2 chip represents a significant leap in Tesla's pursuit of optimizing AI training through its Dojo supercomputer. Both chips are integral to Tesla's strategy, but the D2 chip introduces groundbreaking innovations that push the boundaries of what is possible in high-performance computing.

The D1 chip was Tesla's first foray into custom-designed hardware specifically tailored for AI workloads. As the foundational building block of the Dojo supercomputer, the D1 chip was designed with the primary goal of maximizing parallel processing efficiency. It is a System on a Chip (SoC) that integrates multiple processing cores, memory, and other essential components onto a single piece of silicon. This integration allowed for faster data transfer between components, reduced latency, and increased energy efficiency—all crucial factors in training the complex neural networks required for Tesla's Full Self-Driving (FSD) technology.

One of the key features of the D1 chip was its ability to perform large-scale parallel computations, making it well-suited for the data-intensive tasks of AI training. Tesla's approach with the D1 chip involved combining multiple chips into Dojo tiles, each containing 25 D1 chips, which could then be further integrated into larger computing units like racks and cabinets. This modular design allowed Tesla to scale the system according to its needs, providing a flexible and powerful platform for AI development.

However, while the D1 chip was a significant achievement, Tesla recognized that there were still limitations in its design, particularly when it came to the bottlenecks that can occur when multiple chips are connected together. The physical connections between chips, even within a tile, can slow down data transfer and create inefficiencies that limit the overall performance of the system.

This is where the D2 chip introduces a revolutionary advancement: wafer-scale integration. The D2 chip builds on the foundation laid by the D1 but takes a radically different approach by integrating an entire Dojo tile onto a single wafer of silicon, rather than assembling individual chips into a tile. A silicon wafer is a thin, circular sheet of semiconductor material that serves as the substrate for building multiple chips. Traditionally, these wafers are sliced into individual chips, which are then packaged and connected in a larger system. However, in wafer-scale integration, the entire wafer is used as a single, massive chip.

The shift to wafer-scale integration with the D2 chip eliminates many of the bottlenecks associated with connecting separate chips. By having all the processing units, memory, and interconnects on the same wafer, the D2 chip allows for nearly instantaneous data transfer between different parts of the chip. This design dramatically reduces latency and increases bandwidth, enabling the D2 chip to perform parallel computations even more efficiently than the D1.

Additionally, the D2 chip's wafer-scale design enhances power efficiency by minimizing the energy lost during data transfer. Since all components are integrated onto the same wafer, there are fewer points of resistance, resulting in less energy dissipation. This not only improves the overall performance of the system but also reduces the power consumption, which is a critical factor in maintaining the sustainability of large-scale supercomputers like Dojo.

In terms of scalability, the D2 chip's wafer-scale integration offers a distinct advantage. With the D1 chip, scaling required adding more tiles, each made up of multiple individual chips. While this was effective, it still involved a degree of complexity in connecting and managing these tiles. The D2 chip, on the other hand, simplifies this process by allowing entire tiles to be created on a single wafer, making it easier to scale the system while maintaining peak performance.

In summary, while the D1 chip laid the groundwork for Tesla's AI training capabilities with its advanced parallel processing and modular design, the D2 chip represents a significant evolution in supercomputing technology. By embracing wafer-scale integration, Tesla has been able to overcome the limitations of traditional chip design, achieving higher efficiency, speed, and scalability in the Dojo supercomputer. The D2 chip's innovations position Tesla at the forefront of AI hardware development, enabling the company to continue pushing the boundaries of what is possible in the realm of autonomous driving and beyond.

Wafer-scale processing represents a significant innovation in the field of high-performance computing, offering a fundamentally different approach to designing and manufacturing chips. Traditional chip manufacturing involves slicing a silicon wafer into individual chips, each of which is packaged and used in various computing systems. However, wafer-scale processing takes this a step further by using the entire silicon wafer as a single, integrated chip, vastly expanding the computational power and efficiency of the system.

To understand wafer-scale processing, it helps to visualize the conventional chip-making process. Typically, a silicon wafer, which is about the size of a dinner plate, is etched with patterns that create multiple individual chips. Once these chips are cut from the wafer, they are packaged and connected together in larger systems, such as in the Dojo supercomputer's D1 tiles. While effective, this process introduces certain inefficiencies, particularly in the physical connections between chips, which can create bottlenecks in data transfer and energy loss.

Wafer-scale processing, as utilized in the D2 chip, eliminates these inefficiencies by treating the entire wafer as a single, massive chip. Instead of slicing the wafer into separate pieces, all the processing units, memory, and interconnects are built directly onto the wafer, allowing them to communicate seamlessly without the need for external connections. This approach provides several key advantages:

1. **Elimination of Bottlenecks:** One of the primary benefits of wafer-scale processing is the reduction of bottlenecks that occur when multiple chips are connected. In a wafer-scale chip, all components are integrated on the same piece of silicon, allowing for nearly instantaneous data transfer between different parts of the chip. This results in significantly higher bandwidth and lower latency, which are critical for tasks that require massive parallel processing, such as AI training.

2. **Improved Power Efficiency:** Wafer-scale processing also enhances power efficiency. Traditional chip systems suffer from energy loss due to the resistance in the physical connections between chips. By eliminating these

connections, wafer-scale chips can operate with much lower power consumption, making them more sustainable and cost-effective to run.

3. **Scalability:** Another advantage of wafer-scale processing is its scalability. In traditional systems, scaling up computational power often involves adding more chips or nodes, each of which requires additional connections and infrastructure. With wafer-scale processing, an entire "tile" of computational power is integrated into one wafer, simplifying the process of scaling up and allowing for greater overall system performance.

A parallel example to Tesla's D2 chip in wafer-scale processing is the Cerebras Systems Wafer Scale Engine (WSE), which is also based on wafer-scale integration. Cerebras took the bold step of creating the world's largest chip, built on a single silicon wafer, to specifically address the demands of AI workloads. The Cerebras WSE contains over 400,000 cores and 18 gigabytes of on-chip memory, making it a powerhouse for AI training. Like the D2 chip, the WSE leverages wafer-scale processing to deliver unparalleled performance in terms of speed, efficiency, and scalability.

Cerebras' WSE and Tesla's D2 chip highlight the potential of wafer-scale processing to revolutionize the supercomputing industry. By moving beyond the limitations of traditional chip design, these innovations offer a glimpse into the future of computing, where the boundaries of performance are continually being pushed.

The Future of Dojo

As Tesla advances its Dojo supercomputer with the D2 chip, the implications for the future of AI and Tesla's role in the supercomputing industry are profound. The D2 chip, with its wafer-scale integration, positions Tesla to lead the next generation of AI hardware, offering capabilities that could transform how AI models are trained and deployed.

The D2 chip's increased efficiency and processing power could significantly accelerate the pace of AI development. Faster AI training means that Tesla can iterate on its Full Self-Driving (FSD) models more rapidly, improving accuracy and reliability in less time. This could lead to quicker advancements in autonomous driving technology, potentially bringing fully autonomous vehicles to market sooner than anticipated.

Moreover, the D2 chip's scalability makes it easier for Tesla to expand Dojo's capabilities as its AI demands grow. As Tesla collects more data from its expanding fleet of vehicles, the ability to scale Dojo efficiently will be crucial in maintaining the pace of AI innovation. This scalability also opens the door for Dojo to be used in other AI applications beyond autonomous driving, such as robotics, energy management, and more, positioning Tesla as a leader in multiple fields.

The impact of the D2 chip on the supercomputing industry could extend beyond Tesla. By demonstrating the viability and advantages of wafer-scale processing, Tesla could influence other companies to adopt similar approaches in their own supercomputing efforts. This could lead to a broader shift in the industry, where wafer-scale integration becomes the standard for high-performance computing, especially in AI and machine learning.

Furthermore, Tesla's continued investment in Dojo and the development of advanced chips like the D2 could position the company as a key player in the AI hardware market. Just as Nvidia has become synonymous with GPUs, Tesla could become a major provider of AI-specific computing infrastructure, potentially offering Dojo as a service to other companies and industries. This would not only diversify Tesla's business model but also solidify its influence in the rapidly growing AI ecosystem.

In summary, the D2 chip's innovations in wafer-scale processing are likely to have a far-reaching impact on both Tesla and the broader AI and supercomputing industries. By pushing the boundaries of what is possible with AI hardware, Tesla is not only advancing its own technological capabilities but also setting the stage for the future of AI development on a global scale. As Dojo continues to evolve, it could redefine the landscape of AI training and deployment, with Tesla at the forefront of this exciting new era.

Chapter 6: The Strategic Importance of Dojo

Tesla's Dojo supercomputer represents a cornerstone of the company's long-term strategy, aiming to transform the landscape of AI training and development. As Tesla continues to push the boundaries of what artificial intelligence can achieve, Dojo is envisioned as the critical infrastructure that will propel these advancements forward.

Tesla's long-term vision for Dojo is not confined to enhancing its Full Self-Driving (FSD) capabilities; rather, it encompasses a broader ambition to revolutionize AI training across multiple domains. The supercomputer is designed to handle the immense data processing needs of Tesla's AI models, enabling faster and more efficient training. This capacity is essential for refining the neural networks that power autonomous vehicles, but it also has applications far beyond the automotive industry. Tesla envisions Dojo as a platform that could be leveraged for a wide range of AI-driven innovations, from robotics and energy management to healthcare and beyond.

At the heart of this vision is Tesla's commitment to vertical integration, a strategy that has been central to the company's success. By developing its own supercomputer, Tesla can optimize every aspect of the AI training process, ensuring that Dojo is perfectly aligned with the company's specific needs. This level of control allows Tesla to innovate more rapidly, reduce costs, and avoid the limitations imposed by relying on third-party solutions. In the long run, Dojo could become a foundational technology for Tesla, driving advancements in AI that maintain the company's competitive edge in an increasingly AI-driven world.

However, the path to realizing this vision is fraught with challenges. The development and deployment of Dojo are complex undertakings, requiring cutting-edge engineering, extensive testing, and substantial financial investment. Building a supercomputer from the ground up is no small feat, and the technical hurdles involved are significant. Tesla must navigate these challenges while ensuring that the system performs at the high levels required for AI training. Any delays or setbacks in the development process could have ripple effects on Tesla's broader AI initiatives, potentially slowing down the company's progress toward full autonomy.

Another major challenge Tesla faces with Dojo is its continued reliance on Nvidia's GPUs. While Dojo is intended to reduce Tesla's dependence on external hardware, the transition to using Dojo exclusively will take time. Nvidia's GPUs remain integral to Tesla's current AI infrastructure, and the company has invested heavily in this technology. Balancing the integration of Dojo with the ongoing use of Nvidia hardware is a logistical challenge that requires careful planning and execution. Additionally, Tesla must ensure that its AI capabilities are not disrupted during this transition, which adds another layer of complexity to the project.

Beyond the technical and logistical challenges, Tesla also faces the inherent risks associated with being a pioneer in AI hardware development. The field of AI is rapidly evolving, and there is always the possibility that new technological breakthroughs could outpace or render certain aspects of Dojo's design obsolete. Tesla must remain agile, continuously innovating and adapting Dojo to keep up with the latest advancements in AI. This requires ongoing investment and a willingness to pivot quickly in response to emerging trends.

Despite these challenges, the potential rewards of Dojo are immense. One of the most significant benefits is the potential for substantial cost savings. By developing its own supercomputer, Tesla can avoid the high costs associated with purchasing and maintaining large quantities of third-party GPUs. Over time, these savings could amount to hundreds of millions of dollars, making Dojo a financially prudent investment.

In addition to cost savings, Dojo promises to significantly enhance Tesla's AI training capabilities. The supercomputer's advanced architecture, including wafer-scale integration and parallel processing, allows it to handle larger datasets and more complex models than traditional systems. This means that Tesla can train its AI models faster and with greater accuracy, accelerating the development of technologies like Full Self-Driving. The ability to process vast amounts of data in real-time is crucial for refining these models, which directly impacts the performance and safety of Tesla's autonomous vehicles.

Moreover, Dojo provides strategic advantages that extend beyond immediate cost savings and performance improvements. By building its own AI training infrastructure, Tesla strengthens its position as a leader in AI and autonomous technology. This technological leadership not only enhances Tesla's brand but also attracts top talent, investors, and partners who want to be associated with cutting-edge innovation. Furthermore, the potential to offer Dojo as a service to other companies opens up new business opportunities and revenue streams, diversifying Tesla's portfolio and reducing its reliance on the automotive sector.

In summary, Dojo is a strategic investment that has the potential to revolutionize AI training and development, both within Tesla and across various industries. While the journey to realize this vision is fraught with risks and challenges, the potential rewards are substantial, offering Tesla significant cost savings, enhanced AI capabilities, and strategic advantages in the rapidly evolving world of AI technology. As Dojo continues to evolve, it could redefine the boundaries of what is possible in AI development, solidifying Tesla's role as a key player in the global AI ecosystem.

Chapter 7: The Broader Impact of Dojo on AI

Advancements in AI supercomputing, such as those represented by Tesla's Dojo, are poised to have far-reaching impacts across a variety of industries beyond automotive. While Dojo is primarily designed to enhance Tesla's Full Self-Driving (FSD) capabilities, its potential applications extend into numerous other sectors where the processing of massive datasets and the training of complex AI models are crucial.

In the healthcare industry, for example, AI supercomputing could revolutionize diagnostics and treatment planning. AI models trained on large datasets of medical images, patient records, and genetic information could significantly improve the accuracy and speed of diagnoses, leading to more personalized and effective treatments. Supercomputers like Dojo could enable the rapid analysis of these vast amounts of data, identifying patterns and correlations that would be impossible for human researchers to detect on their own. This could lead to breakthroughs in understanding diseases, developing new drugs, and tailoring treatments to individual patients' genetic profiles.

In finance, AI supercomputing could enhance risk assessment, fraud detection, and investment strategies. Financial institutions rely on analyzing large datasets to predict market trends, assess risks, and make investment decisions. A supercomputer like Dojo could process these datasets in real-time, allowing for more accurate predictions and faster responses to market changes. Additionally, AI models trained on transaction data could improve fraud detection systems, identifying suspicious activity with greater precision and reducing the likelihood of false positives.

The field of energy management is another area where AI supercomputing could have a profound impact. As the world shifts towards renewable energy sources, the management of energy grids becomes increasingly complex. AI models that can predict energy demand, optimize the distribution of resources, and integrate renewable sources into the grid are essential for ensuring stability and efficiency. Supercomputers like Dojo could enable real-time monitoring and optimization of energy systems, helping to reduce waste, lower costs, and improve the reliability of energy supplies.

However, as AI supercomputing continues to advance and influence various industries, it also raises significant ethical considerations. The power of AI to analyze and act on vast amounts of data presents both opportunities and risks, particularly when it comes to privacy, security, and the potential for bias in AI decision-making.

One of the primary ethical concerns is the potential for AI systems to infringe on individual privacy. Supercomputers like Dojo can process and analyze enormous datasets, including personal information, with unprecedented speed and accuracy. While this capability can lead to valuable insights and innovations, it also raises the risk of privacy violations. For instance, AI models trained on large datasets of personal information could be used to make decisions that impact individuals' lives, such as determining creditworthiness or assessing health risks, without their knowledge or consent. This underscores the need for robust data protection regulations and ethical guidelines to ensure that AI is used responsibly.

Another ethical issue is the potential for bias in AI models. AI systems are only as good as the data they are trained on, and if that data contains biases—whether related to race, gender, socioeconomic status, or other factors—those biases can be reflected and even amplified in the AI's decisions. Supercomputers like Dojo, which are capable of training highly complex models, could inadvertently perpetuate these biases on a large scale. It is essential for companies developing AI technologies to implement measures to identify and mitigate bias, ensuring that AI systems are fair and equitable.

The role of supercomputers like Dojo in the development of autonomous systems also raises ethical questions about accountability and decision-making. As AI systems become more autonomous and capable of making decisions without human intervention, it becomes increasingly important to establish clear guidelines for accountability. For example, in the context of autonomous vehicles, questions arise about who is responsible when an AI-driven vehicle makes a decision that leads to an accident. Addressing these ethical dilemmas requires careful consideration and the development of frameworks that balance innovation with public safety and trust.

Looking ahead, the future of AI supercomputing is likely to be shaped by a combination of technological advancements, competitive dynamics, and emerging trends. As AI continues to evolve, so too will the demands placed on supercomputing systems, driving the need for even more powerful, efficient, and scalable solutions.

One potential area of innovation is in quantum computing, which could revolutionize the field of AI by providing a new level of computational power. Quantum computers operate on principles that are fundamentally different from traditional computing, allowing them to solve certain types of problems much faster than classical computers. While quantum computing is still in its early stages, its potential to accelerate AI training and processing could eventually surpass even the most advanced supercomputers like Dojo.

Another emerging trend is the development of edge computing, where AI processing is performed closer to the source of data—such as on devices themselves—rather than in centralized data centers. This approach reduces latency and allows for real-time processing, which is particularly valuable for applications like autonomous vehicles and IoT (Internet of Things) devices. As edge computing becomes more prevalent, supercomputers like Dojo may need to integrate with these decentralized systems to provide seamless AI processing across different environments.

In terms of competition, other tech giants and startups are likely to continue developing their own AI supercomputing solutions, each with unique capabilities and strengths. Companies like Google, with its Tensor Processing Units (TPUs), and Cerebras, with its wafer-scale engines, are already pushing the boundaries of AI hardware. The competition in this space will drive innovation, leading to more specialized and efficient AI supercomputing systems that cater to the specific needs of different industries.

Overall, the advancements in AI supercomputing, epitomized by Tesla's Dojo, are set to transform industries far beyond automotive, introducing new capabilities and ethical challenges. As these technologies evolve, the future of AI supercomputing will be shaped by the convergence of quantum computing, edge computing, and continued innovation in AI hardware, ensuring that supercomputers like Dojo remain at the cutting edge of technological progress.

Conclusion

Tesla's journey in developing the Dojo supercomputer is a testament to the company's unwavering commitment to innovation and its bold vision for the future of artificial intelligence. The concept of Dojo was born out of necessity—a recognition that existing supercomputing solutions were insufficient to meet the growing demands of AI training, particularly in the context of Tesla's Full Self-Driving (FSD) technology. From its inception, Dojo was envisioned as more than just another supercomputer; it was conceived as a revolutionary tool that would allow Tesla to push the boundaries of AI development and achieve its ambitious goals of full autonomy.

The development of Dojo was not without its challenges. Building a supercomputer from the ground up required Tesla to leverage its expertise in vertical integration and first principles thinking. Every aspect of Dojo, from its custom-designed D1 and D2 chips to its innovative wafer-scale architecture, was meticulously crafted to optimize AI training for Tesla's specific needs. This journey involved overcoming significant technical hurdles, navigating the complexities of hardware design, and making substantial financial investments. Yet, through determination and a relentless pursuit of excellence, Tesla has brought Dojo from a bold concept to a tangible reality that is poised to redefine the landscape of AI supercomputing.

Looking ahead, the impact of Dojo on Tesla's future and the broader AI landscape could be profound. Dojo's ability to process massive datasets with unparalleled speed and efficiency could accelerate the development of Tesla's FSD technology, bringing the company closer to realizing its vision of fully autonomous vehicles. But the potential applications of Dojo extend far beyond the automotive industry. As AI continues to permeate every aspect of modern life, from healthcare to finance to energy management, Dojo's capabilities could be leveraged to drive innovation across multiple sectors, positioning Tesla as a leader not just in electric vehicles, but in AI technology as a whole.

Moreover, the development of Dojo represents a strategic shift for Tesla, allowing the company to reduce its reliance on external hardware suppliers and take control of its AI training infrastructure. This move towards greater vertical integration could result in significant cost savings, improved efficiency, and a stronger competitive position in the rapidly evolving AI space. As Dojo continues to evolve, it could also open up new business opportunities for Tesla, such as offering AI training as a service to other companies, further diversifying the company's revenue streams and expanding its influence in the global technology landscape.

In reflecting on the risks and rewards of pioneering new technology, it becomes clear that Tesla's journey with Dojo is emblematic of the challenges and opportunities that come with pushing the boundaries of what is possible. The development of

Dojo has required Tesla to navigate uncharted territory, take bold risks, and invest heavily in a vision that is not guaranteed to succeed. There are inherent uncertainties in developing such cutting-edge technology, from the technical complexities involved to the rapidly changing nature of the AI field itself. Yet, it is precisely this willingness to embrace risk that has defined Tesla's success and positioned the company as a trailblazer in multiple industries.

The rewards of successfully developing and deploying Dojo could be immense. If Dojo lives up to its promise, it could not only transform Tesla's AI capabilities but also set new standards for the entire industry. Tesla's ability to innovate at this level could inspire other companies to push the envelope in their own AI endeavors, driving further advancements in the field and accelerating the pace of technological progress. Moreover, the lessons learned from developing Dojo could inform future projects, both within Tesla and beyond, contributing to the ongoing evolution of AI and supercomputing.

In conclusion, Tesla's development of the Dojo supercomputer represents a bold bet on the future of AI. It is a project that embodies the company's core values of innovation, risk-taking, and a relentless pursuit of excellence. While the journey has been fraught with challenges, the potential rewards are extraordinary. Dojo is not just a tool for advancing AI; it is a symbol of Tesla's commitment to shaping the future. As the world continues to grapple with the implications of AI and its role in society, Tesla's work with Dojo serves as a powerful reminder that the future belongs to those who dare to dream big and take bold action to turn those dreams into reality.

www.ingramcontent.com/pod-product-compliance
Lightning Source LLC
LaVergne TN
LVHW051606050326
832903LV00033B/4385